EGGPLANT

Designed by Eddie Goldfine
Layout by Ariane Rybski
Edited by Catriel Lev and Sorelle Weinstein
Photography by Danya Weiner
Elan Penn 7

Library of Congress Cataloging-in-Publication Data Available

2   4   6   8   10   9   7   5   3   1

Published by Sterling Publishing Co., Inc.
387 Park Avenue South, New York, NY 10016
© 2007 by Penn Publishing Ltd.
Distributed in Canada by Sterling Publishing
c/o Canadian Manda Group, 165 Dufferin Street,
Toronto, Ontario, Canada M6K 3H6
Distributed in the United Kingdom by GMC Distribution Services,
Castle Place, 166 High Street, Lewes, East Sussex, England BN7 1XU
Distributed in Australia by Capricorn Link (Australia) Pty. Ltd.
P.O. Box 704, Windsor, NSW 2756, Australia

Sterling ISBN-13: 978-1-4027-3999-6
ISBN-10: 1-4027-3999-0

For information about custom editions, special sales, premium and
corporate purchases, please contact Sterling Special Sales
Department at 800-805-5489 or specialsales@sterlingpub.com.

EGGPLANT

More than 75 Delicious Recipes

OFIR JOVANI

PHOTOGRAPHY BY DANYA WEINER

STERLING

New York / London
www.sterlingpublishing.com

TABLE OF CONTENTS

DISCOVERING EGGPLANT

INTRODUCTION

What fruit can be big or small, round or oblong? What fruit can be white, green, yellowish, purple, or purple-black with an off-white spongy flesh? The versatile eggplant, of course. This fruit comes in many different colors, shapes, and sizes. Eggplant (or aubergine, as it is called in France and Italy) is actually originally native to southern India and Sri Lanka. The eggplant made its way from India to the Middle East, and since then it has been transplanted throughout the world. When the Arabs conquered Spain in the twelfth century, the eggplant traveled to Europe and impacted heavily on European cuisine. It was in fact Thomas Jefferson who introduced eggplant to this country, but it has only been in the last hundred years or so that eggplant has been regarded as more than simply an ornament or table decoration.

Nowadays, health-conscious people who are experimenting with vegetarian cuisine welcome this delicious option; the fleshy texture and bulk of eggplant compensate for the absence of meat in many dishes. There are believed to be over a thousand different ways to prepare eggplant. To name just some of the methods that appear in this cookbook, eggplant can be sautéed, baked, broiled, grilled, roasted, stuffed, and stewed — making this fruit a major ingredient in many kitchens worldwide. In this cookbook, you will encounter the joys of cooking with eggplant and discover how it can enrich and invigorate appetizers, soups, quiches, main courses, and even pasta sauces and jam.

Ofir Jovani

NUTRITIONAL INFORMATION

Eggplant does not excel in any particular vitamin or mineral, but like most vegetables, it has few calories, is extremely filling, and has practically no fat. The main benefit of eggplant is its high fiber content. These characteristics, along with the meaty texture of the eggplant, make it an ideal vegetarian entrée.

TIPS

SELECTING EGGPLANT

Eggplant is available all year long, though the peak season is usually from July to October; and most of the crop in the United States comes from Florida, though the states of New Jersey and California are also producers of eggplants.

The most well-known type of eggplant in this country is the dark purple, oval (or pear-shaped) variety, though you can also find the 6–8-inch-long white eggplant, which usually has firmer, moister flesh than the purple eggplant, in many stores and specialty markets.

In addition, there is a range of miniature varieties, including the small, dark purple, round or oval type known as baby eggplant, which we use here in several recipes. The smaller varieties tend to have thinner skins and fewer seeds, and are usually sweeter and tenderer than the larger types of eggplant. When picking an eggplant, try to find one which is well rounded and symmetrical with smooth, uniformly colored skin, since discolorations, bruises, and scars on the skin of the eggplant may be indications of decay; the stem and the cap of the eggplant should be bright green. It is also recommended to avoid an eggplant whose skin looks wrinkled or flabby, since it will probably taste bitter, and to avoid light-feeling ones which may be woody. A fresh eggplant will "bounce back" from your touch, the indentation made by your finger pressing against it quickly refilling. The recommended diameter for a young, sweet, and tender eggplant is 3–6 inches; ones which are larger may be bitter or too tough.

IDEAL TEMPERATURE

The ideal temperature for storing an eggplant is about 50°, since excess cold or heat will damage it. Be careful not to puncture the skin of the eggplant or bruise it when storing it, since this can lead to decay. If there is enough space in your refrigerator without having to force it to fit in, an uncut, unwashed eggplant should last for three or four days in a plastic bag in the crisper of your refrigerator; but if you force it into a tight space, you may damage it, bringing on decay.

PREPARATION

Make sure to wash the eggplant just before you are ready to prepare the recipe and use a stainless steel knife to cut off the cap and the stem. Washing the eggplant too early may increase the decay, while using other types of knife (such as a carbon steel blade, which will blacken it) may discolor it. We often list in our recipes eggplant strips or "finger" slices, which refer to the pieces that result when you cut up the eggplant into sticks of approximately equal size, resembling straight French fries, about ½ inch thick (in some of the recipes we give a different thickness, as appropriate).

SALTING

In several of the recipes here, we call for salting the eggplant before cooking, baking, or frying it. Our general rule is that an eggplant should always be salted before deep-frying; this is in order to drain off some of the water from the eggplant and give a denser texture to its flesh, causing it to absorb less fat and give off less water during cooking. Salting the eggplant also tends to reduce its natural bitterness, though precooking the eggplant in boiling water can also be used for this purpose. Of course, once the salting is completed, you should shake the salt off the eggplant (or rinse it off) to avoid carrying along any of the water or bitterness which the salt may absorb. Anyone on a sodium-restricted diet should consult his or her doctor or dietician before using any recipe which involves salting the eggplant.

APPETIZERS AND SOUPS

GRILLED EGGPLANT STEAKS WITH BALSAM-OREGANO SAUCE

Enjoy this classic Italian antipasto appetizer with bread, sliced tomatoes, and a choice ripe cheese.

INGREDIENTS

Serves 4–6

2 medium eggplants, diced ½ inch

½ cup olive oil

2 oregano sprigs

¼ cup balsamic vinegar

2 cloves garlic, thinly sliced

Pinch of coarse salt

PREPARATION

1. Spread the olive oil thinly over the slices.

2. Place the slices on a grill or in the oven at 350°F until brown and soft.

3. Mix together all the remaining ingredients in a bowl to make the sauce.

4. Pour the sauce over the eggplant slices, and serve at room temperature.

EGGPLANT AND RED PEPPER TERRINE

This is a perfect dish for a long hot summer's day.

INGREDIENTS

Serves 2

1 medium eggplant, sliced lengthwise into thin slices

Coarse salt for salting eggplant

Cooking oil

1 red pepper

Filling:

⅔ cup goat's milk cream cheese

4 tablespoons gorgonzola cheese

8 basil leaves, chopped

Pinch of caraway seeds

PREPARATION

1. Sprinkle coarse salt over the eggplant slices, and let sit for 20 minutes.

2. Shake the eggplant slices well to remove any salt or fluid from them.

3. Lightly brown the slices on both sides in a frying pan with a small amount of oil, and leave to drain on paper towels.

4. Roast the red pepper in the oven at 400°F, scorching the skin.

5. Place the pepper in a sealed container; cool it and remove the skin.

6. Mix all the filling ingredients together in a bowl.

7. Line a terrine or deep soup bowl with enough plastic wrap to cover twice the interior surface area of the terrine (with the excess hanging over the edges).

8. Arrange the eggplant slices so that they completely cover the interior surface of the terrine and stick out a bit beyond the top of the terrine. Set 2 to 3 slices aside for later use.

9. Spread half the filling in an even layer over the eggplant slices in the terrine.

10. Top that layer with the red pepper, and spread the remaining filling over it.

11. Cover with the edges of the eggplant slices that stick out and with the slices that were set aside.

12. Close the plastic wrap tightly around all the edges and the top, and place a heavy plate on top to weigh it down.

13. Cool overnight in the refrigerator, then slice it while cold before serving.

14. This recipe can be stored in the refrigerator for up to 4 days.

TOMATO AND DILL EGGPLANT SLICES

Serve this light, refreshing dish cold with a fresh cheese platter and enjoy a summer specialty.

INGREDIENTS

Serves 3–4

1 large eggplant, sliced ½ inch thick

Coarse salt for salting eggplant

Cooking oil

1 cup fresh tomatoes, crushed

2 tablespoons fresh dill, chopped

Juice of 1 lemon

1 teaspoon crushed garlic

PREPARATION

1. Sprinkle coarse salt over the eggplant slices, and set aside for 20 minutes.

2. Shake the eggplant slices well to remove any salt or fluid from them.

3. Fry the eggplant in oil until brown and soft. Remove from pan and set on paper towels to drain.

4. To prepare the sauce, in a large bowl mix the tomatoes, dill, lemon juice, and garlic.

5. Set a layer of eggplant on a serving dish and pour on a layer of sauce. Continue to layer eggplant and sauce until both are gone.

MOCK CHOPPED LIVER

This recipe tastes remarkably similar to the real thing, without the cholesterol of real liver.

INGREDIENTS

Serves 4

1 medium eggplant, sliced lengthwise

Cooking oil

2 onions, diced

2 hard-boiled eggs

1 tablespoon soy sauce

½ teaspoon salt

Pinch of black pepper, finely ground

PREPARATION

1. Spread the oil thinly over the eggplant slices, and bake in the oven at 350°F until completely browned and softened.

2. Fry the diced onion in a small amount of oil in a frying pan until caramel-brown.

3. Blend the eggplant, onions, eggs, and all the other ingredients in a food processor, and refrigerate for 30 minutes.

4. Serve chilled or at room temperature.

LEMON-MINT EGGPLANT SALAD

This salad, which is excellent with toast, is also tasty when accompanied by lettuce.

INGREDIENTS

Serves 4

1 quart (4 cups) cooking oil

Coarse salt for salting eggplant

2 medium eggplants, diced 1 inch

½ cup lemon juice

3 slices pickled lemon

1 teaspoon garlic, crushed

2 shallots, finely chopped

leaves of 6 mint sprigs, coarsely chopped

½ teaspoon salt

Pinch of ground black pepper

PREPARATION

1. Preheat the oil in a deep pan.

2. Sprinkle coarse salt over the eggplant slices, and let sit for 30 minutes.

3. Shake the eggplant slices well to remove any salt or fluid from them.

4. Fry the eggplant in the oil over a medium to high flame to brown and soften.

5. Mix the lemon juice, pickled lemon, garlic, onions, mint, salt, and pepper together in a bowl.

6. Add the eggplant to the bowl containing the mixture.

7. Refrigerate for 1 hour to allow the eggplant to absorb the flavor from the mixture.

8. Serve cold.

THAI EGGPLANT SALAD

You can store this tasty salad in the refrigerator for up to 2 weeks.

INGREDIENTS

Serves 4

2 medium eggplants, roasted and peeled

1 tablespoon sesame oil

4 tablespoons teriyaki sauce (or 3 tablespoons soy sauce and 1 tablespoon mirin or honey)

3 tablespoons lime juice, lemon juice, or rice vinegar

2 cloves garlic, crushed

1 hot pepper, seeded and finely chopped

3 tablespoons olive oil

4 tablespoons coriander and/or parsley, finely chopped

Salt to taste

Freshly ground black pepper to taste

PREPARATION

Rinse the eggplant and place in a large bowl. Add the rest of the ingredients and mash together until uniform. Taste and add pepper and/or salt if necessary.

CHEESE QUARTET EGGPLANT ROLLS

This deliciously fun treat is appropriate for cocktail parties or just a simple nighttime snack!

INGREDIENTS

Makes 5 rolls

1 large eggplant, sliced lengthwise into thin slices

Coarse salt for salting eggplant

Cooking oil

Filling:

⅔ cup goat's milk cream cheese

⅓ cup Roquefort cheese

⅓ cup Parmesan cheese, grated

4 tablespoons mozzarella cheese

Handful of basil, chopped

4 teaspoons olive oil

1 scallion, chopped

Pinch white pepper

PREPARATION

1. Sprinkle salt evenly over the eggplant slices, and let set for 10 minutes.

2. Shake off salt, and any fluid drawn out by it, from eggplant slices.

3. Pour 1 inch of oil into a wide frying pan and heat.

4. Fry both sides of the eggplant slices until brown, and leave to drain on paper towels.

5. Stir all the filling ingredients in a bowl until a well-mixed homogeneous mass is formed.

6. Place 3 slices of eggplant side by side with no space between them on a sushi mat.

7. Pour the filling into a piping bag, and squeeze it out across the width of the eggplant slices.

8. Roll the eggplant slices up around the filling (as you would with sushi).

9. Repeat steps 6–8 until all the eggplant slices are used up.

10. Cool in the refrigerator for at least 30 minutes.

11. Remove from the refrigerator, cut each roll into ¾-inch pieces, and serve.

PICKLED BABY EGGPLANTS

This is my grandmother's recipe for pickled eggplants. As children, we would spend many a happy afternoon enjoying this tasty snack.

INGREDIENTS

Makes 30

30 baby eggplants for pickling

1 quart (4 cups) wine vinegar or natural white vinegar

4 cups water

1½ tablespoons salt

1 bunch parsley, with stalks removed

leaves from 1 bunch basil

1 bunch coriander, with stalk removed

25 cloves garlic, peeled

¼ teaspoon ground dried chili

PREPARATION

1. Wash off each baby eggplant and cut a groove in it lengthwise along most of its length, but not to the very end.

2. Arrange the baby eggplants in a wide pot and pour the vinegar, water, and salt over them.

3. Bring to a boil, and then cook over a medium flame for 10 minutes to soften the eggplants slightly.

4. Strain the eggplants from the pot, saving the liquid separately and cooling it.

5. Puree the parsley, basil, coriander, garlic and chili together in a food processor.

6. Insert some puree into the grooves of each of the baby eggplants, and place them in a sterile jar.

7. Pour the liquid from step 4 over the eggplants in the jar, and refrigerate for 3 days.

8. Serve cold or at room temperature. These pickles can be stored in the refrigerator for several weeks.

EGGPLANT TABBOULEH

A traditional Middle Eastern salad with a delightful twist.

INGREDIENTS

Serves 6

2 medium eggplants, sliced lengthwise

Coarse salt for salting eggplant

Olive oil for cooking

½ pound coarse bulgur wheat

4 scallions, thinly sliced

¼ cup red wine vinegar

1 sweet red pepper, diced ¼ inch

2 tablespoons raisins

¼ cup dill, chopped

½ teaspoon dried chilies, ground

½ teaspoon cardamom, ground

½ teaspoon dried coriander, ground

½ teaspoon cloves, ground

½ teaspoon dried ginger, ground

½ teaspoon nutmeg, ground

PREPARATION

1. Sprinkle coarse salt over the eggplant slices, and let sit for 20 minutes.

2. Shake the eggplant slices well to remove any salt or fluid from them.

3. Fry the eggplant in olive oil until soft and golden brown. Transfer to paper towels to drain.

4. Rinse the burghul and place in a large bowl. Cover with boiling water and set aside for 30 minutes.

5. Fluff the burghul with a fork. If there is still liquid in the bowl, drain off the excess liquid before fluffing.

6. Add the eggplant and the remaining ingredients. Mix well. Set aside for 30 minutes. Serve at room temperature.

EGGPLANT FUSILLI WITH TAPENADE OF OLIVES AND RICOTTA CHEESE

This dish is excellent served cold as a pasta salad, at a picnic or garden party.

INGREDIENTS

Serves 4

2 medium eggplants, diced 1-inch

Cooking oil

1 pound uncooked fusilli pasta

2 tablespoons garlic, crushed

¼ cup olive oil

¾ cup black olive tapenade

20 fresh basil leaves, coarsely chopped

2 tomatoes, cut into large cubes

1 teaspoon salt

1 cup ricotta cheese, crumbled

Basil leaves for garnish

PREPARATION

1. Coat the eggplant pieces evenly with cooking oil and place in a large baking dish in one layer. Bake at 350°F for 20 minutes until brown and soft.

2. Cook the pasta according to the package directions and drain.

3. In a large frying pan, fry the garlic in olive oil until it is golden brown.

4. Add the tapenade, eggplant, pasta, basil, tomatoes, and salt, and toss lightly.

5. Spread the cheese over the pasta and mix gently. Remove from the heat, garnish with more basil leaves, and serve immediately.

INDONESIAN EGGPLANT SALAD

This recipe, originating from the Indonesian kitchen, is characterized by the flavor of coriander, honey, and garlic. For those who prefer a less spicy salad, a red pepper may be substituted for the chili pepper.

INGREDIENTS

Serves 4

2 medium eggplants, diced
1 inch

Cooking oil

Sauce:

3 tablespoons honey

2 tablespoons soy sauce

⅓ cup coriander, finely chopped

1 tablespoon coriander seeds, roasted and crushed

1 teaspoon fresh garlic, crushed

1 fresh chili pepper, chopped

PREPARATION

1. Deep-fry the diced eggplant in a pan preheated to medium heat until golden brown.

2. Leave to drain on paper towels.

3. Mix together the sauce ingredients in a bowl.

4. Add the fried eggplant, and mix well.

5. Allow the eggplant to absorb the sauce for several minutes before serving.

ROMANIAN EGGPLANT SALAD

Sample a taste of Romania in this deliciously rich eggplant salad.

INGREDIENTS

Serves 4

2 large eggplants

1 red pepper

1 green pepper

1 small red onion

2 pickles

⅓ cup parsley, chopped

½ cup canola oil

¼ cup vinegar

1 teaspoon coarse salt

PREPARATION

1. Scorch the eggplant over an open flame, or by grilling in a frying pan, until the meat is fully softened.

2. Leave to cool on a plate.

3. Dice the peppers, onion, and pickles, and place them in a deep bowl.

4. Cut around the edges of the eggplant with a knife to separate the meat from the peel.

5. Gently scoop out the meat with a spoon, and add to the bowl of diced vegetables.

6. Add the parsley, canola oil, vinegar, and salt.

7. Mix together all the ingredients with a fork until an even consistency is achieved.

8. Serve immediately or let set for a few hours to improve flavor.

EGGPLANT MOZZARELLA FALAFEL

These tempting appetizers appear to be tasty falafel balls from the outside, but inside is an explosion of creamy mozzarella surrounded by crispy eggplant.

INGREDIENTS

Makes 24 balls

Balls:

3 medium eggplants, peeled and sliced ½ inch

Olive oil for brushing

½ cup Parmesan cheese, grated

½ cup kashkaval cheese, grated (you may substitute provolone or mozzarella cheese)

¼ cup parsley, chopped

1 egg

¼ cup breadcrumbs

Salt to taste

Freshly ground black pepper to taste

24 balls baby mozzarella, or 2 large balls cut into cubes

Coating:

1 cup breadcrumbs

½ cup unroasted hazelnuts, shelled and coarsely ground

1 egg, beaten with a tablespoon of water

Cooking oil

PREPARATION

1. Preheat oven to 350°F.

2. Arrange eggplant slices on a baking sheet that is covered with baking paper. Brush with olive oil and bake for 20 minutes. Turn the slices over carefully, brush with olive oil, and bake for another 15 minutes until golden. Remove from oven and set aside to completely cool.

3. Transfer the eggplant to a food processor. Process with short pulses to a coarse consistency. Add the Parmesan, kashkaval, parsley, and egg, and pulse until mixed but not liquid. Transfer to a large bowl, add the bread-crumbs, and mix well. Add salt and pepper to taste. Refrigerate for 2 hours until the mixture is settled.

4. After the eggplant mixture has cooled, form the balls. Roll a small amount of the mixture in your hand to form a 2-inch ball. Gently flatten the ball in the palm of your hand and place a baby mozzarella ball in the center. Gather the sides and roll the ball to cover the cheese. Repeat with the rest of the mixture.

5. Mix together the breadcrumbs and hazelnuts. Place mixture in a bowl. Place the egg in a bowl and dip each ball in the egg and then in the coating. Place the balls on a tray and refrigerate. At this point you may store the balls in the freezer before frying.

6. Heat the oil in a deep skillet. Fry the balls until they are brown on all sides. It is a good idea to fry one ball first, separately, to test that the oil is not too hot. If the oil is too hot, the outside will fry too quickly and the cheese inside will not melt. Fry for 2–3 minutes. Remove from the skillet and transfer to paper towels to drain for a few seconds before serving.

BREADED EGGPLANT ON BEET GREENS

This exquisite recipe should be prepared shortly before serving in order to retain its crispiness.

INGREDIENTS

Serves 3–4

2 eggs, beaten

1 cup breadcrumbs

1 medium eggplant, sliced into thin (¼-inch) slices

Oil for greasing the baking pan

1 lemon, thinly sliced

½ teaspoon coarse salt

1 bunch beet greens

½ cup olive oil

2 tablespoons butter

1 teaspoon garlic, crushed

PREPARATION

1. Pour the eggs into a bowl and the breadcrumbs onto a plate.

2. Dip the eggplant slices into the beaten egg mixture, and then coat with breadcrumbs; perform twice for each eggplant slice.

3. Grease a baking pan with oil, and spread the lemon slices side by side along the bottom of the pan.

4. Place the eggplant slices on top of the lemon slices, leaving small gaps between the eggplant slices.

5. Spread the coarse salt evenly over the eggplant slices.

6. Bake in the oven for about 30 minutes at 350°F until golden brown.

7. Scald the beet greens for 1 minute and soak in cold water.

8. Pour the olive oil into a frying pan and heat over a high flame.

9. Add the butter and garlic, and fry lightly.

10. Add the beet greens and sauté lightly.

11. Spread the beet greens on a serving tray, and place the eggplant slices on top of the leaves.

12. Garnish with the lemon slices before serving.

SPICY SALSA EGGPLANT

Serve this spicy concoction with tortillas and cheese.

INGREDIENTS

Serves 4–6

2 medium eggplants, sliced lengthwise into ¾-inch slices

Cooking oil

½ cup olive oil

1 onion, diced

1 red pepper, with seeds removed, thinly sliced

5 cloves garlic, sliced

½ cup tomato paste

1 teaspoon hot/sweet paprika

2 tomatoes, diced

Pinch of salt

2 basil sprigs, thinly sliced

PREPARATION

1. Deep-fry the eggplant slices until brown and soft.

2. Remove from the frying pan and leave to drain on paper towels.

3. Pour the olive oil into a deep-frying pan over a medium flame, and lightly brown the onion and the red pepper.

4. Add the garlic and fry lightly, while adding the tomato paste and paprika. Stir well.

5. Add the tomatoes and salt and continue frying for 10 more minutes, with the frying pan covered.

6. Add the eggplant and basil, and stir gently.

7. Remove from the flame and allow to cool. Serve at room temperature.

TOASTED EGGPLANT AND BROCCOLI FLORET SALAD

Impress your guests with this festive salad, which can be served either as a tasty appetizer or as a colorful addition to a main course.

INGREDIENTS

Serves 4–5

1 medium eggplant, diced 1 inch

1 cup olive oil

2 large red peppers

½ cup pine nuts, roasted

¾ cup tamarind sauce

1 tablespoon Worcestershire sauce

1 teaspoon salt

Pinch of black pepper

⅔ cup baby shrimp

Oil for sautéing

1 broccoli floret, separated from the stalk

2 cups alfalfa sprouts

1 scallion, coarsely chopped

PREPARATION

1. Spread half of the olive oil lightly over the diced eggplant, and arrange in a baking pan.

2. Cut the peppers into thin strips and arrange in another baking pan.

3. Bake both pans in the oven for 25 minutes at 350°F, and remove from the oven.

4. Blend the remaining olive oil, peppers, half the pine nuts, tamarind sauce, Worcestershire sauce, and salt and pepper at top speed in a food processor until a smooth, homogenous textured pepper sauce is produced.

5. Sauté the baby shrimp in a frying pan in a small amount of cooking oil.

6. In a deep bowl, gently mix the eggplant, broccoli, shrimp, and alfalfa sprouts together with the pepper sauce.

7. Serve on a tray after garnishing with the scallion and the remaining pine nuts.

EGGPLANT PESTO

This colorful and delicious dish may be served hot as a main course or cold as a pasta salad appetizer.

INGREDIENTS

Serves 4–5

1 large eggplant, diced ½ inch

⅓ cup olive oil

½ teaspoon coarse salt

1 cup dried tomatoes, softened in oil

One cup feta cheese, diced

½ cup Parmesan cheese, grated

10 basil leaves, chopped

One-pound package penne pasta

4 heaping tablespoons pesto

Basil leaves for garnishing

PREPARATION

1. Combine the eggplant, oil, and salt, and place in a baking pan.

2. Bake in the oven for 20 minutes at 350°F.

3. Coarsely chop the tomatoes and place in a bowl together with the cheeses and the chopped basil leaves.

4. Cook the pasta according to instructions on the package (usually 12 minutes in twice its volume of water).

5. Strain and cool in cold water.

6. Add the pasta, pesto, and eggplant to the bowl containing the other ingredients, and stir gently.

7. Garnish with basil leaves and serve.

BABA GANOUSH

Serve this classic Middle Eastern appetizer as a dip with tortilla chip or pita bread.

INGREDIENTS

Serves 4

2 medium eggplants

¼ cup lemon juice

½ teaspoon salt

3 tablespoons tahini paste

Handful of parsley, thinly chopped

½ cup olive oil

PREPARATION

1. Preheat the oven to 400°F. Prick the eggplants all over with a fork.

2. Bake the eggplants for 30 minutes until tender.

3. Remove from the oven; halve the eggplants and scoop out the meat.

4. Add lemon juice and blend in a food processor until a smooth consistency is achieved.

5. Add salt and tahini paste to the eggplant mixture and combine all the ingredients.

6. Set aside to cool and stir in the parsley.

7. Before serving, drizzle olive oil over the eggplant.

EGGPLANT CROSTINI

A fantastic hors d'oeuvre for a cocktail party, this appetizer is served on bite-sized pieces of toast.

INGREDIENTS

Serves 4

2 large eggplants

⅓ cup olive oil

10 slices of bread, cut into 1½-inch squares

2 red tomatoes

2 hard-boiled eggs

3 heaping tablespoons mayonnaise

1 teaspoon garlic, crushed

½ cup parsley, chopped

1 teaspoon salt

⅓ cup garden cress, coarsely chopped

PREPARATION

1. Scorch the eggplants well on all sides over an open flame, or in a frying pan with a thick bottom over a high flame, to thoroughly soften the meat and char the peel.

2. Scoop out the eggplant meat and place in a bowl.

3. Lightly spread the olive oil over the pieces of bread.

4. Toast in the oven for 10 minutes at 325°F to crisp, then cool.

5. Coarsely grate the tomatoes and eggs and add to the bowl containing the eggplant.

6. Add the mayonnaise, garlic, parsley, and salt, and stir well to produce the spread.

7. Arrange a few garden cress leaves on each piece of toast.

8. Place a heaping teaspoon of spread on top of the garden cress on each piece of toast (you may need a second spoon to keep the spread from spilling).

9. Serve at room temperature.

EGGPLANT AND ROASTED PEPPER MUFFINS

These tasty muffins are a healthy snack or a terrific side dish for any meal.

INGREDIENTS

Makes 8 medium-sized muffins

1 medium eggplant, cubed

Coarse salt for salting eggplant

Cooking oil

2 red peppers, roasted, seeded, peeled, and cubed

1 cup cake flour

½ teaspoon baking soda

1 cup cornstarch (not instant)

Salt to taste

Freshly ground black pepper to taste

1 cup sweet cream

2 ounces butter, melted

1 egg

3½ ounces kashkaval cheese, grated (you may substitute provolone or mozzarella cheese)

½ cup dill, chopped (optional)

PREPARATION

1. Sprinkle coarse salt over the eggplant, and let sit for 20 minutes.

2. Rinse the eggplant well to remove any salt or fluid.

3. Heat oil in a skillet and fry the eggplant cubes until golden brown. Remove from the skillet and place on a paper towel to drain.

4. Place the peppers in a colander and set aside to allow the liquid to drain.

5. Place the peppers and eggplant in a bowl and mix.

6. Preheat the oven to 400°F.

7. Place the flour, baking soda, cornstarch, salt, and pepper in a large bowl and mix well. Add the sweet cream, butter, egg, and cheese and mix well.

8. Pour the mixture into the muffin cups in a muffin pan. Fill each cup ¾ full and put in a little of the eggplant and pepper mixture. Garnish the top of each muffin with a little dill (optional).

9. Bake for 25 minutes until a toothpick inserted in the center comes out clean. Remove from the oven and allow the muffins to cool. Remove from the pan and serve warm.

EGGPLANT FRITTATA

A Frittata is an unfolded omelet, and is often finished under the broiler. You can substitute your favorite vegetables and cheeses for those used in this recipe.

INGREDIENTS

Serves 4

½ medium eggplant, sliced into ½-inch slices

Coarse salt for salting eggplant

Cooking oil for frying

2 small shallots, chopped

1 tablespoon butter

5 eggs, beaten

¼ cup sweet cream

½ cup crumbled salted cheese

1 tablespoon Parmesan cheese, grated

2 scallions, chopped

Pinch of crushed black pepper

PREPARATION

1. Sprinkle coarse salt over the eggplant slices, and let sit for 20 minutes.

2. Shake the eggplant slices well to remove any salt or fluid from them.

3. Deep-fry the eggplant slices until brown and soft.

4. Leave to drain on paper towels.

5. Lightly fry the shallots in a frying pan with butter, until translucent.

6. In a bowl, mix the eggs, cream, and cheeses together, and pour into the frying pan.

7. Pour the eggplant, scallion, and pepper on top, and stir gently.

8. Bake in the oven for 15 minutes at 350°F, and serve hot.

EGGPLANT MAYONNAISE SALAD

Discover the joys of preparing your own mayonnaise in this classic recipe. For a quick and easy salad, use store-bought mayonnaise instead of making your own.

INGREDIENTS

Serves 4

1 large eggplant

1 teaspoon garlic, crushed

Mayonnaise:

2 egg yolks

2 level teaspoons Dijon-style mustard

1 cup olive oil

2 tablespoons wine vinegar

1 teaspoon salt

½ teaspoon ground pepper

PREPARATION

1. Leave out the mayonnaise ingredients until they reach room temperature.

2. Scorch the eggplant over an open flame until completely soft.

3. Peel off the skin and leave the meat of the eggplant in a bowl.

4. Place the egg yolks and the mustard in a round bowl and whisk together until they reach a uniform texture.

5. Gradually mix in the oil until it is completely absorbed.

6. Gently stir in the vinegar, salt, and pepper.

7. Add the mayonnaise and the garlic to the eggplant.

8. Stir gently to combine, and serve cool or at room temperature.

SPICY MOROCCAN EGGPLANT SALAD

This spicy dish is a wonderful spread on pita or toasted bread and can even be served with Middle Eastern couscous for an exotic entrée.

INGREDIENTS

Serves 4

3 medium eggplants

12 cloves garlic, whole

1 hot green pepper, seeded and sliced into thin rings

1 dried red hot pepper, seeded and sliced into thin rings

3½ tablespoons olive oil

3 teaspoons ground cumin

1 teaspoon sweet paprika

2 cloves garlic, crushed

Salt to taste

2 teaspoons sugar

3½ tablespoons vinegar

PREPARATION

1. Using a sharp knife, score the eggplants lengthwise 8–10 times on each eggplant. Insert the whole garlic and the pepper slices into the scores.

2. Steam the eggplants in a covered steamer until soft (around 1 hour).

3. Allow the eggplants to cool to room temperature and use a sharp knife or a mandoline to slice the eggplants into thin slices. Place the sliced eggplant in a bowl.

4. Heat the olive oil in a heavy-bottomed skillet or large sauce-pan. Add the cumin, paprika, crushed garlic, salt, and sugar and briefly sauté for 30 seconds.

5. Add the eggplant slices and stir gently. Remove skillet from the heat, add the vinegar, and lightly mix. Serve cold or at room temperature. Store for up to 5 days.

EGGPLANT AND POMEGRANATE SALAD

The combination of eggplants and pomegranates make this salad a unique and tasty treat, but the sour cream gives it an extra special "kick".

INGREDIENTS

Serves 8

3 medium eggplants, scorched and peeled

Seeds of 1 pomegranate

Juice of 1 pomegranate

2 tablespoons basil, chopped

3 tablespoons dill, chopped

1 clove garlic, crushed

Salt to taste

Freshly ground black pepper to taste

1 cup sour cream

PREPARATION

1. Scoop the meat of the eggplant into a large glass bowl.

2. Add the pomegranate seeds, pomegranate juice, basil, dill, garlic, salt, and pepper. Mix gently until well blended and set aside to cool.

3. Add the sour cream and mix well.

4. It is advisable to store the salad in the refrigerator overnight so the flavors become mingled and evenly distributed.

5. Stir before serving.

EGGPLANT-YOGURT SOUP

This refreshing soup recipe originally derives from Greece, where it is known as Tzatziki.

INGREDIENTS

Serves 4–5

1 medium eggplant, cut into ½-inch strips

½ cup olive oil

4 cups plain yogurt

2 cucumbers, diced ½ inch

1 dill sprig, finely chopped

1 scallion, finely chopped

¾ cup cold water

½ teaspoon salt

½ teaspoon ground white pepper

leaves from 2 mint sprigs (to be used for garnishing), finely chopped

PREPARATION

1. Spread half the olive oil over the eggplant strips.

2. Bake in the oven for 20 minutes at 350°F to brown and soften.

3. Whisk together well all other ingredients (except the remaining olive oil and mint leaves) in a bowl.

4. Add the eggplant strips and mix gently.

5. Cool in the refrigerator for 30 minutes.

6. Garnish with mint leaves, sprinkle the remaining olive oil on top, and serve.

EGGPLANT-CHICKEN DIM SUM

A dumpling-like dish from the Chinese kitchen, dim sum *goes best with traditional sauces of Asian origin.*

INGREDIENTS

Serves 4

Dough:

2 cups flour

1 egg

½ cup warm water

Filling:

1 medium eggplant, diced ½ inch

Oil for baking

1½ cups chicken, ground

1 teaspoon fresh ginger, finely chopped

1 egg

⅓ cup scallions, chopped

1 teaspoon Worcestershire sauce

2 tablespoons soy sauce

¾ cup breadcrumbs

Miscellaneous:

3–5 lettuce leaves

PREPARATION

1. Knead the dough ingredients together well.

2. Let the dough set for 30 minutes, and knead again.

3. Mix the diced eggplant with a small amount of oil and bake at 350°F for 20 minutes.

4. Mix well with the remaining filling ingredients.

5. Roll out the dough into a thin layer, and cut into squares.

6. Place 1 tablespoon of filling in the center of each square, and fold dough over it.

7. Place the dim sum on the lettuce leaves in a steamer.

8. Steam for 25 minutes and serve hot.

Option: Instead of steaming the dim sum with lettuce leaves, eliminate the lettuce and deep-fry in oil.

EGGPLANT WITH SESAME SAUCE

This salad is particularly appropriate for serving with pasta or spread over an assortment of lettuce leaves.

INGREDIENTS

Serves 4

2 medium eggplants, peeled and cut into ½-inch "finger" slices

½ cup olive oil

1 tablespoon sesame seeds

1 teaspoon black sesame seeds

4 tablespoons sesame oil

1 thyme sprig, finely chopped

⅓ teaspoon coarse salt

PREPARATION

1. Spread the olive oil generously and evenly over the eggplant slices.

2. Bake for 20 minutes in a baking pan lined with baking paper, in an oven preheated to 350°F.

3. Roast the sesame seeds and the black sesame seeds with the sesame oil for 1 minute in a frying pan over a high flame.

4. Remove from the flame and add the thyme.

5. Place the eggplant slices on a serving platter.

6. Pour the sesame seeds, oil, and thyme over them, sprinkle salt on top, and mix gently.

7. Leave to set for at least 1 hour (a three to four hour wait is preferable).

8. Serve cold.

EGGPLANT WITH SILAN SAUCE

This appetizer is sensational when served alongside tahini sauce or low-fat white cheese, which accents the gentle sweetness of the eggplant. The silan sauce itself can be purchased in glass jars in many food stores.

INGREDIENTS

Serves 4

½ cup flour

1 teaspoon sesame seeds

¼ teaspoon pepper, crushed

Pinch of salt

1 medium eggplant, sliced into ½-inch slices

Coarse salt for salting eggplant

2 eggs, beaten

Cooking oil

Sauce:

¼ cup red wine

½ cup silan (date honey) sauce

1 tablespoon vinegar

PREPARATION

1. Mix the flour, sesame, pepper, and salt in a bowl.

2. Sprinkle coarse salt over the eggplant slices, and let sit for 20 minutes.

3. Shake the eggplant slices well to remove any salt or fluid from them.

4. Coat the eggplant slices with eggs, then dredge them with the flour mixture from the bowl.

5. Deep-fry the eggplant slices on both sides until golden brown, and leave to drain on paper towels.

6. To make the sauce, pour the wine, silan sauce, and vinegar into a frying pan, and cook while stirring for 10 minutes over a medium flame.

7. Arrange the eggplant slices on a serving platter and pour sauce over them evenly before serving.

EGGPLANT ARTICHOKE SALAD

The contrast between the soft and creamy eggplant and the crunchy artichoke hearts creates a delicious, tantalizing salad.

INGREDIENTS

Serves 4–6

2 artichokes

½ lemon

2 medium eggplants, diced ½ inch

4 cloves garlic, sliced

½ onion, chopped

½ cup olive oil

1 teaspoon coarse salt

½ teaspoon sweet/hot paprika

PREPARATION

1. Wash off the artichokes and place in a deep pot.

2. Squeeze the juice from the lemon half onto the artichokes, and fill the pot with enough water to cover the artichokes.

3. Bring to a boil and cook for 30 minutes over a medium flame.

4. Remove the artichokes from the pot and cool.

5. Separate the leaves from the artichoke hearts, and save for later. Remove the hair-like strands from the artichoke hearts, and dice the hearts.

6. Combine the eggplant, artichoke, garlic, and, and mix together with olive oil (leaving a small amount for later) and salt in a wide baking pan.

7. Bake in the oven preheated to 350°F for 30 minutes.

8. Remove from the oven and cool.

9. Arrange the artichoke leaves on a serving tray, and place the baked eggplant-artichoke mix on top.

10. Sprinkle on the paprika and the remaining olive oil, and serve.

EGGPLANT GAZPACHO

Though most believe that the main ingredient of gazpacho is tomatoes, gazpacho really descends from an ancient Spanish dish based on a combination of stale bread, garlic, olive oil, salt, and vinegar — in essence, a cold bread soup.

INGREDIENTS

Serves 4–6

Gazpacho:

10 ripe red tomatoes with seeds removed, coarsely chopped

3 red peppers, coarsely chopped

½ onion, coarsely chopped

4 cloves garlic

2 cucumbers, coarsely chopped

½ cup olive oil

1 teaspoon salt

Miscellaneous:

1 medium eggplant, diced 1 inch

1 tablespoon coarse salt

Cooking oil

2 cloves garlic, sliced

3 tablespoons olive oil

1 tablespoon balsamic vinegar

2 tablespoons Worcestershire sauce

2 tablespoons soy sauce

4–6 toasted bread slices

⅓ cup scallions, chopped

PREPARATION

1. Grind all the gazpacho ingredients well in a food processor, until an even, but coarse, consistency is achieved.

2. Refrigerate for at least 2 hours.

3. Sprinkle coarse salt over the eggplant slices, and let sit for 20 minutes.

4. Shake the eggplant slices well to remove any salt or fluid from them.

5. Deep-fry the eggplant until softened and browned.

6. Leave to drain on paper towels.

7. Lightly fry the garlic slices in a frying pan with the olive oil until golden brown.

8. Add the vinegar, Worcestershire sauce, and soy sauce, along with the fried eggplant.

9. Mix well and remove from the flame.

10. Pour some gazpacho into a bowl, and place a piece of toast into it.

11. Scoop about a tablespoon of the eggplant mixture onto the center of the toast.

12. Garnish with chopped scallions.

13. Repeat steps 10 to 12 until all servings are prepared, then serve.

QUICHES
AND
BAKED
ENTRÉES

EGGPLANT-GOAT CHEESE QUICHE

This sumptuous quiche will not only make a good entrée, but will also transform a light supper into something special.

INGREDIENTS

Serves 4–6

Pastry crust:

2 cups flour

1 egg

Approximately ¼ pound butter, diced ½ inch

1 teaspoon salt

3 tablespoons cold water

Filling:

2 medium eggplants

Juice of half a lemon

2 cloves garlic, chopped

¼ teaspoon salt

¼ cup olive oil

2 eggs, beaten

½ cup sour cream

½ cup goat's milk cream cheese

4 scallions, chopped

¼ cup Parmesan cheese, grated

PREPARATION

1. Knead the pastry crust ingredients for just enough time to produce the dough.

2. Line a 12 x 10-inch baking pan with the dough, and bake in the oven for 12 minutes at 350°F.

3. Scorch the eggplants to soften the meat, then scoop out the meat and mince.

4. Combine all of the filling ingredients, except for the Parmesan cheese and the eggplants.

5. Mix the minced eggplant meat together with all of the combined filling ingredients, except for the Parmesan cheese, and pour into the baking pan on top of the dough.

6. Sprinkle the Parmesan cheese evenly over the filling.

7. Return to the oven for another 25 minutes at 350°F.

8. Serve hot.

EGGPLANT MINI-QUICHE

A rich, crispy pastry shell filled with tender eggplant makes a heavenly appetizer.

INGREDIENTS

Serves 4–6

Dough:

2 cups flour

1 egg

3½ ounces cold butter, cubed

1 teaspoon salt

2–3 tablespoons cold water as needed

Filling:

2 medium eggplants, roasted, meat removed and coarsely chopped

Juice from half a lemon

2 cloves garlic, chopped

Salt to taste

½ cup olive oil

1 medium eggplant, sliced into 8–10 slices

Coarse salt for salting eggplant

Olive oil for cooking

½ pound goat cheese or feta cheese, cubed

10 basil leaves, chopped

2 eggs

1 cup sweet cream

2 onions, sliced

3–4 tablespoons demerara sugar

Small amount of sweet red wine

PREPARATION

1. Knead the ingredients for the dough together. Do not over-knead the dough or your crust will be tough.

2. For the filling, mix together the chopped eggplant, lemon juice, garlic, salt, and olive oil in a large bowl. Set aside.

3. Sprinkle coarse salt over the eggplant slices, and let sit for 20 minutes.

4. Shake the eggplant slices well to remove any salt or fluid from them.

5. Fry the eggplant slices in olive oil. Cut the slices into cubes and add to the eggplant mixture. Add the cheese and the basil and mix well.

6. Beat the eggs and the cream together in a separate bowl. Set aside.

7. Lightly sauté the onions in olive oil until they are golden. Add the sugar and continue to cook until the onions begin to caramelize. Add the wine and continue to cook until the mixture becomes smooth.

8. To assemble one mini-quiche, place the dough in a quiche pan and press down with your fingers. Decorate the top edge of the dough with a fork. Spoon a layer of caramelized onion in the bottom of each quiche. Pour the filling on top of the onions. Repeat the process for each mini-quiche. Bake for 350°F for 30 minutes or until the quiche is lightly browned.

EGGPLANT-CHEESE BOUREKAS

Bourekas are among the delicious group of small, stuffed pastries served in the Mediterranean as appetizers, hors d'oeuvres, and even at street stands.

INGREDIENTS

Makes 8–10 bourekas

2 large eggplants, diced ½ inch

½ cup olive oil

2 mashed potatoes

2 eggs, beaten

½ pound (approximately 2 cups) cheddar cheese, diced

¼ cup coriander, chopped

1 teaspoon turmeric

1 teaspoon salt

¼ cup flour

1 pound pastry dough

Oil for greasing baking pan and coating bourekas

1 egg yolk

2 tablespoons sesame seeds

PREPARATION

1. Spread oil evenly over the diced eggplant, and bake in the oven for 25 minutes at 350°F.

2. Remove from the oven and cool.

3. To make the filling, mix the mashed potatoes, eggplant, eggs, cheese, coriander, turmeric, and salt together in a bowl.

4. Dust a working surface with flour, and roll out the dough to a ¼-inch thickness.

5. Cut the dough into 3-inch wide strips.

6. At the end of each strip, place about 1½–2 tablespoons of filling.

7. Fold the strips of dough over the filling into triangles, enclosing the filling in a double thickness of dough, and cut off any excess dough.

8. Grease a baking pan with oil and arrange the bourekas in it.

9. Beat the egg yolk together with some oil, and apply it to the bourekas with a pastry brush.

10. Sprinkle sesame seeds on top of the bourekas, and bake in an oven preheated to 350°F for about 25 minutes, until they rise and brown.

11. Serve hot.

EGGPLANT-MOZZARELLA QUICHE

Serve with a fresh garden salad for a delicious Sunday brunch.

INGREDIENTS

Serves 4–6

Pastry crust:

2 cups flour

1 egg

Approximately ¼ pound butter, diced ½ inch

1 teaspoon salt

3 tablespoons cold water

Filling:

1 small eggplant, diced

Coarse salt for salting the eggplant

¾ cup sweet cream

4 egg yolks

¼ cup mozzarella cheese, grated

Oil for deep frying

PREPARATION

1. Knead the pastry crust ingredients for just enough time to produce dough.

2. Line a 12 x 10-inch baking pan with the dough, and bake in the oven for 12 minutes at 350°F.

3. Sprinkle coarse salt over the eggplant slices, and let sit for 25 minutes.

4. Shake the eggplant slices well to remove any salt or fluid from them.

5. Deep-fry the eggplant until lightly browned.

6. Leave to drain on paper towels.

7. Mix the eggplant together with all of the filling ingredients, and pour into the baking pan on top of the dough.

8. Return to the oven for another 25 minutes at 350°F.

9. Serve hot.

PARMESAN PASTRY WTH EGGPLANT FILLING

For this recipe, you may prepare the dough in advance and freeze it for later use.

INGREDIENTS

Serves 8

Pastry:

2½ cups organic flour

½ cup all-purpose flour

7 ounces unsalted margarine, softened

¾ cup sour cream

¼ cup Parmesan cheese, finely grated

Filling:

2 medium eggplants

Salt to taste

Freshly ground black pepper to taste

1 tablespoon thyme, chopped

1¾ ounces ricotta cheese

1 egg yolk

PREPARATION

1. Mix together all the ingredients for the pastry in a large bowl and set aside in the refrigerator overnight.

2. Preheat the oven to 350°F.

3. Roast the eggplant until it is soft under an open flame. Scoop out the meat of the eggplant into a large bowl.

4. Add the remaining ingredients except for the egg and mix well.

5. Thinly roll out the pastry and cut it into squares. Place a small amount of filling in the middle of each pastry square and fold over to create either a triangle or a square depending on your taste. Brush some egg yolk over the edges before pressing them down to seal.

6. Brush egg yolk on the top of each pastry and bake for 30 minutes or until golden brown.

EGGPLANT FILO DOUGH PASTRY

Filo dough is a thin, versatile pastry dough which is popular in the Balkans. This type of dough is sold in frozen rolls which must be defrosted before use. It is preferable to refrigerate filo dough overnight so that it doesn't break apart during use.

INGREDIENTS

Serves 4–6

2 small eggplants, sliced into long strips, ½ inch thick

¼ cup olive oil

½ teaspoon coarse salt

1 onion, chopped

Oil for frying

½ cup gorgonzola cheese or blue cheese, crumbled

½ cup ricotta cheese

10 basil leaves, chopped

½ teaspoon caraway seeds

1 egg

2 tablespoons roasted pine nuts

¼ cup butter

2 rolls filo dough, each about 20 inches long

Oil for greasing baking pan and coating pastries

1 tablespoon sesame seeds

PREPARATION

1. Spread oil liberally over the eggplant strips and sprinkle salt on top.

2. Bake in the oven for 20 minutes at 350°F.

3. Brown the onion in a frying pan with a small amount of oil.

4. Mix the cheeses, basil, caraway seeds, onion, egg, and pine nuts together in a bowl to make the filling.

5. Melt the butter and use it to connect the two rolls of filo dough.

6. Cut the dough into 5-inch squares.

7. Drop 1 tablespoon of filling into the center of each square of dough.

8. Cut the eggplant strips into pieces, and place one piece on top of the filling on each square of dough.

9. Fold the squares of dough to envelop the filling.

10. Grease a baking pan with oil, and place the pastries in it.

11. Apply oil to each pastry with a pastry brush.

12. Sprinkle sesame seeds on top, and bake in an oven preheated to 350°F for 15 minutes.

13. Serve hot.

EGGPLANT MEAT FOCACCIA

The word "focaccia" is derived from the Latin word Focus, *which means
"hearth." This simple flat bread, shaped as a rustic slab or round, was named in
the days when it was baked by Etruscans on a hot stove over the embers of a fire
in Northern Italy.*

INGREDIENTS

Serves 10

Dough:

8 cups (3 pounds) flour

3 tablespoons sugar

1½ tablespoons salt

4½ tablespoons dry yeast

1½ cups lukewarm water

2 eggs

⅓ cup olive oil

Filling:

2 large eggplants, sliced into
1-inch slices

Coarse salt for salting the
eggplant slices

Oil for frying

2 onions, chopped

⅓ cup olive oil

2 cups ground beef

Miscellaneous:

Additional flour for use when
needed

Oil for greasing baking pan

1 tablespoon hot paprika

1 teaspoon fresh ground
oregano

leaves from 5 rosemary sprigs

1 tablespoon coarse salt

PREPARATION

DOUGH:

1. Mix 5⅓ cups of flour with the
sugar, salt, and yeast in a bowl.

2. Gradually mix in the water.

3. Add the eggs and knead for 10
minutes.

4. Sprinkle the remaining flour
over the work area and knead the
dough there, allowing the dough
to absorb the flour. (Add more
flour if the dough is too watery.)

5. Add olive oil to the dough and
continue to knead until it is
absorbed.

6. Cover the dough with a damp
cloth, and leave to rise for 45
minutes.

(continued on page 68)

(continued from page 66)

FILLING:

7. Sprinkle coarse salt over the eggplant slices, and let sit for 20 minutes.

8. Shake the eggplant slices well to remove any salt or fluid from them.

9. Fry eggplant slices in oil until lightly brown.

10. Leave the eggplant slices to drain on paper towels.

11. Brown the onions in olive oil in a frying pan.

12. Add the ground beef and cook for about 10 minutes while crumbling the beef.

13. Once the beef is cooked, add paprika.

14. Cook for about 2 more minutes to complete the meat filling, and remove from the flame.

15. Once the dough has risen, divide it up into 10 portions, and roll into balls.

16. On a work area sprinkled with flour, roll out the dough into thin flat circles.

17. Grease the baking pan with oil, and place dough circles on it.

18. Spread the meat filling, eggplant slices, paprika, oregano, rosemary, and coarse salt evenly over the dough circles.

19. Bake in the oven for 30–35 minutes at 325°F until the dough is golden brown.

20. Serve hot.

SMOKED GOOSE ROLLS WITH MUSHROOM AND EGGPLANT

This savory pastry has an amazingly enticing aroma and is best served warm and fresh from the oven.

INGREDIENTS

Serves 4–6

Dough:

1 pound flour

1½ ounces yeast

1 egg

1 tablespoon sugar

1 teaspoon salt

6 tablespoons olive oil

1½ cups water, lukewarm

Filling:

3½ ounces smoked goose breast or bacon

Cooking oil

3½ ounces wild mushrooms

2 medium eggplant, scorched, peeled, and coarsely chopped

1 cup scallions, chopped

2 cloves garlic, crushed

1 teaspoon tarragon

Salt to taste

White pepper to taste

1 teaspoon fresh ginger, grated

1 egg

1 tablespoon soy sauce

1 egg, beaten, for brushing pastry

PREPARATION

1. To prepare the dough, place all the ingredients for the dough in a food processor with a kneading hook. Add the water last. Process until the dough is soft and smooth. Cover the dough and allow it to rise until it doubles in volume. Knead the dough for five minutes and set it aside to rise again.

2. To prepare the filling, fry the goose breast in a small amount of oil for 2–3 minutes until crispy. Remove the goose and set aside. Do not empty the skillet of the oil from the goose. Cook the mushrooms in the same pan for 2–3 minutes until just tender. Place the mushrooms and goose in a large bowl.

3. Add the rest of the ingredients for the filling and mix well.

4. Preheat the oven to 350°F.

5. After the dough has risen a second time, roll it out to a ¼-inch-thick rectangle.

6. Spread the filling on the dough evenly but leave some space around the edges. Roll the dough into a cylinder. Slice the dough into 1½–2-inch-thick slices. Arrange the slices in a flower shape in a round pan lined with baking parchment. You may also bake the slices individually on a regular baking sheet without forming a flower shape. Brush the tops of the rolls with the beaten egg.

7. Bake for 20 minutes until they are nicely browned.

MEAT AND FISH ENTRÉES

STUFFED EGGPLANT

This delicious dish is easy to prepare; you can substitute white rice, or another grain, for the brown rice in this recipe.

INGREDIENTS

Serves 4

5 large tomatoes

2 cups ground beef, mixed with a small amount of lamb fat

1 teaspoon cumin

1 teaspoon turmeric

1 level teaspoon salt

½ cup brown rice cooked in water (prepared like pasta)

2 medium eggplants, halved widthwise

Pinch of pepper

½ cup olive oil

PREPARATION

1. Mash the tomatoes and pass them through a strainer.

2. Season the beef with cumin, turmeric, and a small amount of salt and mix with the rice.

3. Cut into each eggplant half, extract some of the flesh (to be used afterwards), and leave a hollow space for the filling.

4. Season the hollow space with the remaining salt and pepper, stuff with the beef and rice mixture, and cover with the extracted eggplant flesh.

5. Pour the olive oil into a pot and add the mashed tomatoes.

6. Add the stuffed eggplants to the pot, cover, and cook over a low flame for 40 minutes.

7. Transfer the stuffed eggplants to a serving platter, pour the liquid from the pot over them, and serve hot.

EGGPLANT PAELLA

Paella, a very popular Spanish dish, which we present here with seafood, is rice seasoned with vegetable sauce. The dish is named after the two-handled pan, also called paella, in which it's prepared and served. The pan is wide and shallow and measures 13 to 14 inches in diameter.

INGREDIENTS

Serves 4–6

⅓ cup olive oil

10 cloves garlic, sliced

1 medium eggplant, diced ½ inch

½ cup shrimp

1 cup calamari meat, sliced into rings

½ cup calamari heads

½ cup crabmeat

2 cups rice

3 tablespoons white wine

1 teaspoon salt

½ teaspoon black pepper, crushed

5 tomatoes, diced ½ inch

4–5 cups fish stock

PREPARATION

1. Pour olive oil into a wide, deep frying pan, and fry the garlic until golden brown.

2. Add the diced eggplant and continue to fry while stirring for 5 minutes.

3. Mix in the shrimp, calamari, crabmeat, and rice and fry for 5 minutes over a medium flame.

4. Add the wine, salt, pepper, and tomatoes, and pour in the fish stock, so that the liquid rises about ½ inch above the rice.

5. Bring to a boil, mixing well; then cover tightly, reduce the flame, and cook over a low flame for 20 minutes.

6. Turn off the flame and leave to set in covered frying pan for 5 minutes before serving.

EGGPLANT BOLOGNAISE LASAGNA

This mouthwatering recipe is a great favorite among children.

INGREDIENTS

Serves 6–9

1 cup olive oil

2 onions, chopped

3 cups ground beef

6 cups tomatoes, crushed

1 tablespoon fresh oregano, chopped

2 tablespoons parsley, chopped

1 teaspoon thyme

2 tablespoons basil

2 medium eggplants, sliced into ¼-inch slices

Coarse salt for salting eggplant

Oil for frying and baking

½ cup mozzarella cheese, grated

½ cup Parmesan cheese, grated

One-pound package of lasagna noodles

PREPARATION

1. In a deep-frying pan, heat up the olive oil and fry the onions until browned.

2. Add the ground beef and cook, while crumbling the beef with a wooden spoon.

3. When the ground beef is cooked and separated, add the tomatoes, oregano, parsley, thyme, and basil, and bring to a boil.

4. Cook over a low flame for about 40 minutes to complete the sauce.

5. Sprinkle coarse salt over the eggplant slices, and let sit for 30 minutes.

6. Shake the eggplant slices well to remove any salt or fluid from them.

7. Fry the eggplant slices in oil until browned, and leave to drain on paper towels.

8. Mix the two types of grated cheeses together.

9. Cook lasagna noodles according to package directions. Grease a baking pan, and lay out a layer of lasagna noodles on it.

10. Pour a layer of sauce on top of the noodles, and sprinkle grated cheese over it.

11. Cover with a layer of eggplant slices, and another layer of lasagna noodles on top of the eggplant.

12. Repeat steps 8 and 9 until the sauce is used up.

13. Bake in the oven for 35 minutes at 350°F.

14. Serve hot.

EGGPLANT–LAMB STEW

This dish goes very well with yogurt or tahini sauces.

INGREDIENTS

Serves 4–6

2 medium eggplants, sliced into 1-inch strips

½ cup olive oil for spreading over eggplant

1 onion, coarsely sliced

2 celery stalks, coarsely sliced

⅓ cup olive oil for frying onion and celery

8 cloves garlic, coarsely chopped

1 carrot, grated

2 cups tomatoes, crushed

3 cups vegetable stock

Pinch of ground cinnamon

2 thyme sprigs, chopped

Meatballs:

2 cups ground lamb

3 tablespoons breadcrumbs

2 eggs

1 tablespoon garlic, crushed

1 tablespoon cumin

2 tablespoons ground coriander seeds

½ teaspoon salt

½ teaspoon ground black pepper

PREPARATION

1. Spread olive oil well over the eggplant strips, and bake in the oven for 20 minutes at 350°F.

2. Mix together all of the meatball ingredients in a bowl to form a homogenous mass, and chill in the refrigerator for 20–30 minutes.

3. In a pot, fry the onion and celery in olive oil until lightly browned.

4. Add the garlic and carrot, and quick-fry.

5. Add the crushed tomatoes, vegetable stock, cinnamon, and thyme, bring to a boil, and reduce the flame.

6. Form meatballs about half the size of a fist, place them in the pot, and cook for 20 minutes.

7. Add the eggplant strips to the meatballs and stir gently.

8. Cover the pot, cook over a low flame for 1 hour, and serve hot.

TRADITIONAL GREEK MOUSSAKA

It is highly recommended to serve moussaka the day after you prepare it, as the flavor develops more fully with time; in fact, moussaka can be frozen for up to a month!

INGREDIENTS

Serves 6–8

3 large eggplants, peeled and sliced into ¾-inch slices

Coarse salt for salting eggplant

Oil for frying

1 large onion, thinly chopped

⅓ cup olive oil

4 cups ground beef

1 teaspoon salt

Pinch of pepper

2 tomatoes, diced

Batter made from 2 eggs, beaten well with 1 tablespoon of flour and a pinch of salt and pepper

PREPARATION

1. Sprinkle coarse salt over the eggplant slices, and let sit for 40 minutes.

2. Shake the eggplant slices well to remove any salt or fluid from them.

3. Partially fry the eggplant slices in oil until lightly browned, and leave to drain on paper towels.

4. Fry the onion in olive oil in a frying pan until brown. Mix in the ground beef until fully cooked, and season with salt and pepper.

5. Line the base and walls of a Pyrex baking pan with half of the eggplant slices.

6. Pour the ground beef mixture on top of the eggplant slices, and spread the tomatoes over it.

7. Cover with a layer of the remaining eggplant slices, and pour the batter over that.

8. Cover with aluminum foil and bake in the oven at 350°F for 45 minutes to 1 hour.

9. Remove the aluminum foil and continue baking for another 15 minutes.

10. Serve hot or reheated on the day after its preparation.

ST. PETER'S FISH EGGPLANT BAKE

Rosebuds serve many functions in the kitchen; not only are they an ingredient in herbal teas, but they are also used for cooking and garnishing dishes.

INGREDIENTS

Serves 4

1 medium eggplant, cut into ½-inch slices

Coarse salt for salting eggplant

Oil for frying and greasing baking pan

⅓ cup olive oil

8 cloves garlic, thinly sliced

10 dried rosebuds

¼ cup white wine

½ cup fish stock

Juice of 2 lemons

1 tablespoon soy sauce

Pinch of salt

Pinch of pepper, crushed

8 lettuce leaves

8 St. Peter's Fish (tilapia) fillets

PREPARATION

1. Sprinkle coarse salt over the eggplant slices, and let sit for 20 minutes.

2. Shake the eggplant slices well to remove any salt or fluid from them.

3. Fry the eggplant slices until browned and softened, and leave to drain on paper towels.

4. Pour olive oil into a frying pan, and fry garlic until lightly browned.

5. Add the rosebuds and sauté lightly.

6. Add the wine, fish stock, and lemon juice and bring to a boil.

7. Add the soy sauce, salt, and pepper and cook for 5 minutes over a high flame. Remove from the flame to use as a sauce afterwards.

8. Grease a baking pan with oil and spread the lettuce leaves over it.

9. Arrange the fish fillets on the lettuce leaves so that the skin faces up.

10. Pour sauce from the frying pan over the fillets, and bake in the oven for 20 minutes at 350°F.

11. Spread the eggplant slices on a serving platter, and arrange the fillets on top of them.

12. Pour the juice from the baking pan over the fillets and garnish with rosebuds.

13. Serve hot.

ROAST GOOSE LEGS WITH EGGPLANT IN CARAMEL SAUCE

The fusion of flavors in this impressive dish will make your taste buds explode.

INGREDIENTS

Serves 4–5

8 goose legs

6 baby eggplants

1 onion, cut into quarters

3 fresh celery stalks, coarsely chopped

1 carrot, sliced into thick slices

2 tablespoons soy sauce

4 bay leaves

1¼ cups chicken stock

½ teaspoon crushed black pepper

2 tablespoons honey

Caramel sauce (for preparation, see the recipe for Chinese Eggplant-Beef Fry on page 100)

PREPARATION

1. Mix together all of the ingredients in a large bowl or pot.

2. Pour the caramel sauce over the other ingredients, and cool in the refrigerator for 6 hours.

3. Pour the prepared mixture into a wide baking pan, and bake in the oven at 340°F for 1¼ hours.

4. During the first half of the baking time, cover with aluminum foil.

5. Stir gently during the last half hour of baking.

6. Serve hot.

"ACQUA PAZZA" EGGPLANT STEW

Acqua pazza *means "crazy waters" in Italian and refers to the old custom in Naples of cooking fish in a bath of seawater, wine, olive oil, and tomatoes. Fishermen have used this method of cooking fish for hundreds of years.*

INGREDIENTS

Serves 4–6

1 onion, chopped

½ cup olive oil

8 cloves garlic

2 tablespoons tomato paste

2 medium eggplants, diced

4 tomatoes, scalded

10 pickled capers

Handful parsley, chopped

¾ cup chicken stock

1 tarragon sprig, chopped

1 teaspoon salt

PREPARATION

1. Fry the onion in olive oil until lightly brown.

2. Add the garlic and continue cooking until golden brown.

3. Add the tomato paste and fry lightly while adding the remaining ingredients.

4. Reduce the flame and cover the frying pan. Let simmer for 50 minutes, stirring gently from time to time.

5. Serve hot or at room temperature.

EGGPLANT "LECHO" WITH SALAMI AND PEPPERS

If you are a vegetarian, this aromatic and flavorful Hungarian dish may also be prepared without the salami, and is best when served with bread.

INGREDIENTS

Serves 4

1 large eggplant, sliced into "finger" slices, 1 inch thick

⅓ cup cooking oil

1 medium onion

1 red pepper, thickly sliced

1 green pepper, thickly sliced

5 cloves garlic

15 thin slices salami

Pinch of caraway seeds

1 tablespoon sweet paprika

Handful parsley, chopped

Pinch of white pepper

Pinch of salt

⅓ cup water

PREPARATION

1. Spread oil thinly over the eggplant slices, and bake in the oven for 20 minutes at 350°F.

2. Fry the onion and peppers in oil in a pot over a high flame until medium brown.

3. Add the garlic and quick-fry, reducing the flame.

4. Add the salami and quick-fry while adding caraway, paprika, parsley, pepper, and salt.

5. Add the eggplant slices and water and mix together.

6. Cover the pot and continue cooking for another 10 minutes.

7. Serve hot.

TUNISIAN EGGPLANT "MAFRUM"

Originating in the North African kitchen, Mafrum is particularly appropriate as a main course served with a side dish of couscous.

INGREDIENTS

Serves 6

2 medium eggplants

1 cup whole wheat flour

3 eggs, well beaten

Oil for frying

Filling:

2 cups ground beef

½ cup breadcrumbs

1 teaspoon chicken soup mix

1 teaspoon cumin

1 egg

1 bunch parsley, chopped

1 squash, grated

Sauce:

⅓ cup olive oil

5 cloves garlic, sliced

1 celery stalk, coarsely sliced

½ cup tomato paste

1 tablespoon paprika

3 tomatoes, scalded and sliced

1 teaspoon brown sugar

1 teaspoon soy sauce

1 cup water

Pinch of salt

PREPARATION

1. Place all the filling ingredients in a bowl.

2. Mix well.

3. Chill in the refrigerator for 30 minutes.

4. To prepare the sauce, pour the olive oil into a wide pot.

5. Lightly brown the garlic and celery in the pot.

6. Add tomato paste and paprika, and lightly fry.

7. Add the other sauce ingredients.

8. Cover the pot and cook over a low flame for 40 minutes.

9. To prepare the eggplant, slice the width of the eggplants into slices two fingers high, and scoop out a well for filling in the middle of each slice.

10. Fill each eggplant slice with 3 tablespoons of filling.

11. Coat each slice with egg and then with flour.

12. Lightly brown the slices over a low flame in a deep frying pan (partial deep fry).

13. Pour the sauce into a wide tray, and arrange the eggplant slices in the tray.

14. Bake for 20 minutes at 350°F.

15. Serve hot.

TEMPURA-FRIED EGGPLANT

*You might be surprised to read that tempura is not a Japanese dish, but
actually originates from Portugal and was created there in the 16th century.*

INGREDIENTS

Serves 4

Tempura batter:

2 eggs, beaten

⅔ cup ice water

1 cup flour

Miscellaneous:

1 medium eggplant, sliced into
thin (¼-inch) slices

Coarse salt for salting eggplant

½ cup flour for dredging

Cooking oil

PREPARATION

1. In a bowl, stir the eggs gently while adding in the water.

2. Sprinkle the flour into the bowl while stirring with a whisk or chopstick until a uniform texture is achieved. Do not stir more than necessary.

3. Sprinkle coarse salt over the eggplant, and let sit for 20 minutes.

4. Shake the eggplant slices well to remove any salt or fluid from them.

5. Dredge the eggplant slices in flour, and shake them off.

6. Dip the slices in batter, and shake off gently.

7. Deep-fry the eggplant in a pan preheated to medium heat until golden brown.

8. Leave to drain on paper towels.

9. Serve hot.

EGGPLANT AND SEAFOOD WITH GARAMASSALA SAUCE

Garamassala, which is an Indian spice mixture, may be purchased in spice stores or stores carrying Oriental products. You may also add oysters them to this recipe if you enjoy them.

INGREDIENTS

Serves 4

1 small eggplant, cut lengthwise into ½-inch strips

Oil for frying

1 red pepper, sliced into ½-inch squares

6 cloves garlic, sliced

1 tablespoon garlic, crushed

2 tablespoons garamassala mixture

¼ cup white wine

1 cup fish stock

½ cup mango concentrate

1 cup shrimp

1 cup calamari meat, sliced into rings

½ cup calamari heads

½ cup crabmeat

½ teaspoon salt

½ cup parsley, chopped

PREPARATION

1. Spread a small amount of oil over the eggplant strips, and bake in the oven for 10 minutes at 350°F, until lightly brown.

2. Pour a small amount of oil into a deep frying pan, and fry the pepper until lightly brown. Add the garlic slices and fry until lightly brown.

3. Add the crushed garlic and garamassala and quick-fry.

4. Pour in the wine and stir. Add the fish stock and mango concentrate, and reduce over a high flame for about 5 minutes.

5. Add the eggplant strips, shrimp, calamari (meat and heads), crabmeat, and salt, and mix gently.

6. Reduce the flame and cook for 10 minutes.

7. Place on a serving platter, garnish with parsley, and serve hot.

CHICKEN LIVER AND EGGPLANT IN WINE SAUCE

The sauce in this recipe is also divine when served with chicken breasts and veal scallopini.

INGREDIENTS

Serves 4–6

Wine sauce:

2 cups good quality red wine

½ cup balsamic vinegar

⅓ cup sugar

Eggplant:

2 medium eggplants

½ cup olive oil

½ teaspoon salt

Juice from half a lemon

Miscellaneous:

1 pound chicken livers, whole and cleaned

Oil or butter for cooking

1 mango, peeled and sliced vertically

Salt to taste

Freshly ground black pepper to taste

PREPARATION

1. To prepare the sauce, pour all the ingredients into a saucepan and cook over a medium flame. Cook until the sauce reduces by a third, so that approximately 1 cup remains.

2. To prepare the eggplant, scorch the eggplant over an open flame. Allow the eggplant to cool slightly. Peel the eggplant and finely chop it. In a bowl, mix the eggplant with olive oil, salt, and lemon juice.

3. To prepare the livers, heat oil or butter in a skillet and cook the livers for 3 minutes until they are browned on the outside and pink on the inside. Set aside.

4. To prepare the mango, sauté the mango slices in a skillet with a small amount of oil or butter for 1–2 minutes.

5. To serve, place a spoonful of eggplant in the center of a plate. Place a few livers on top of the eggplant. Add salt and pepper to taste. Arrange 3 slices of mango on the plate and pour the sauce on top.

GRILLED TROUT WITH EGGPLANT

Serve this colorful and aromatic dish with baked potatoes.

INGREDIENTS

Serves 4

1 medium eggplant, diced 1 inch

2 red peppers, cut into 1-inch squares

½ cup olive oil

1 teaspoon salt

4 egg yolks

1 tablespoon breadcrumbs

4 cleaned trouts (each about ¾ pound)

Oil for greasing baking pan

8 rosemary sprigs

2 heads garlic, separated into cloves

1 teaspoon pepper, crushed

PREPARATION

1. Mix the diced eggplant and peppers with the olive oil and a small amount of salt and place in a baking pan.

2. Bake in the oven at 350°F for 30 minutes.

3. Remove from the oven and cool. Mix with egg yolks and breadcrumbs in a bowl.

4. Stuff each trout's belly with the mixture from the bowl.

5. Grease the baking pan with oil, and arrange rosemary leaves (separated from the sprigs) to cover the base of the pan, placing the fish on top.

6. Spread the garlic cloves, pepper, and remaining salt over the fish.

7. Bake in the oven at 350°F for 40 minutes.

8. Serve hot.

EGGPLANT CHICKEN CASSEROLE

When baking this dish in the oven, use a ceramic casserole pot or a thick iron pot.

INGREDIENTS

Serves 4–5

1 large eggplant, sliced into 1-inch slices

Coarse salt for salting eggplant

Oil for frying

1 medium onion, chopped

½ cup olive oil

1 chicken, divided into six pieces

3 cloves garlic, chopped

1 teaspoon turmeric

Pinch of ground clove

1 teaspoon salt

Pinch of pepper

2 cups rice

1½ cups water

½ cup coconut milk

PREPARATION

1. Sprinkle coarse salt over the eggplant slices, and let sit for 20 minutes.

2. Shake the eggplant slices well to remove any salt or fluid from them.

3. Fry the eggplant slices in oil until lightly browned, and leave to drain on paper towels.

4. In a pot, fry the onion in olive oil until browned.

5. Add the chicken and garlic, and quick-fry.

6. Add turmeric, ground clove, salt, pepper, and rice, and stir well.

7. Pour in the water and coconut milk and bring to a boil.

8. Reduce the flame and cover the pot, and cook for 20 minutes.

9. Turn off the flame and leave in the covered pot for 10 minutes.

10. Line the base of the ceramic pot with eggplant slices, and pour the chicken-rice mixture over them.

11. Cover and bake in the oven at 350°F for 40 minutes.

12. Serve hot.

EGGPLANT SALTIMBOCCA

In Italian, Saltimbocca *literally means "it jumps in the mouth"; the combination of mozzarella cheese and bacon in this dish is so tasty that it makes you want this mouthwatering treat to jump into your mouth.*

INGREDIENTS

Serves 4

1 red pepper, sliced into thin strips

¾ cup (½ pound) bacon, sliced into thin strips

Oil for frying

1 medium eggplant, diced ½ inch

Coarse salt for salting eggplant

½ cup mozzarella cheese, grated

½ cup parsley, chopped

½ teaspoon pepper, crushed

Leaves from 2 thyme sprigs

4 pieces of ¼-inch-thick veal scallopini, each approximately 2½ x 2½ inches

½ cup flour

Sauce:

6 cloves garlic, sliced

½ cup olive oil

5 cups tomatoes, crushed

5 basil leaves

Pinch of salt

PREPARATION

1. Fry the red peppers and bacon in oil in a frying pan until lightly browned, and transfer to a bowl.

2. Sprinkle coarse salt over the eggplant slices, and let sit for 20 minutes.

3. Shake the eggplant slices well to remove any salt or fluid from them.

4. Deep-fry the diced eggplant and leave to drain on paper towels.

5. When the eggplant has cooled, add it to the bowl along with the mozzarella cheese, parsley, pepper, and thyme, and mix together to make the filling.

6. Place a piece of scallopini on the counter; spread it out, place 2 tablespoons of the filling from the bowl in the center, and fold over so that it covers the filling and becomes a filled ball of meat. Secure it closed with a toothpick and follow the same procedure for the other pieces of scallopini.

7. Coat each ball of meat with flour, and deep-fry the meat in oil over a medium flame until lightly browned.

8. Bake in the oven for 15 minutes at 325°F.

9. To prepare the sauce, fry the garlic in olive oil in a deep frying pan until golden brown.

10. Add the tomatoes, basil, and salt, and reduce for 10 minutes over a high flame while stirring.

11. Pour the sauce onto a serving platter.

12. Gently remove the toothpicks from the meat, and place the meat on top of the sauce in platter. Serve hot.

ANCHOVY EGGPLANT CASEROLE

For this dish, the most appropriate eggplants are those with few seeds (usually the smaller varieties).

INGREDIENTS

Serves 4–6

2 medium eggplants, peeled

2 cups sweet cream

4 eggs, beaten

4 tablespoons flour

2 onions, diced

Oil for frying

10 fresh brussels sprouts (or 10 frozen brussels sprouts after defrosting), halved

2 anchovy fillets from a can, finely chopped

1 tablespoon chicken soup mix

1 zucchini, grated

1 tablespoon butter, for greasing the baking pan

PREPARATION

1. Put the eggplants in a pot of boiling water and cook for approximately 20 minutes, until they soften.

2. Strain the water from the eggplants and mash them with a fork.

3. Mix the cream and the eggs in a bowl, and gradually mix in the flour.

4. Fry the onions in a small amount of oil in a frying pan until browned, and add to the bowl.

5. Add all the other ingredients, except the butter, to the bowl and mix well.

6. Grease the baking pan with butter, and pour the mixture from the bowl into the baking pan.

7. Bake in the oven for 45 minutes at 325°F.

8. Raise the oven temperature to 350°F and bake for another 10 minutes.

9. Serve hot.

EGGPLANT-STUFFED CALAMARI

Use fresh calamari for this recipe to maximize the flavor.

INGREDIENTS

Serves 3

10 calamari, cleaned

Filling:

1 small eggplant, scorched

4 tablespoons goat cheese

2 tablespoons Parmesan cheese, grated

6 basil leaves

Leaves from 3 sprigs of thyme

Salt to taste

Freshly ground black pepper to taste

3 tablespoons olive oil

4 cloves garlic, chopped

6 wild mushrooms, thinly chopped

½ tablespoon breadcrumbs

PREPARATION

1. To prepare the filling, remove the meat of the eggplant and mash it to a smooth paste. Add the cheeses, spices, salt, and pepper, and mix well.

2. Heat the olive oil in a skillet and briefly cook the garlic and the mushrooms until they are just heated. Sprinkle some breadcrumbs in the skillet to absorb some of the liquid from the mushrooms. Add the eggplant mixture and mix. Set aside in the refrigerator for 30 minutes.

3. Stuff the calamari with the eggplant mixture, ¾ full. Close the calamari with toothpicks. Set the calamari aside until they reach room temperature so that the stuffing does not come out during cooking.

4. At this point, you may prepare the calamari for serving in several ways:

a. Coat each piece with flour and fry in oil, taking care not to allow the calamari to come apart. Serve on a bed of green leaves and balsamic vinegar.

b. Prepare a marinade from olive oil and spices. Brush each calamari with the marinade and roast over an open fire. Baste the calamari while cooking. Serve immediately.

c. Prepare a tomato sauce for the calamari. In a small saucepan, steam tomato cubes and garlic with a small amount of olive oil. Add white wine and salt to taste. Add pepper and parsley to taste. Cook the calamari in the sauce for 30–40 minutes on low heat. Serve hot.

PORK OSSO BUCCO WITH EGGPLANT

Osso bucco literally means "bone hole" in Italian; the dish comes sliced in such a way that the bone and its marrow are in the center of the meat.

INGREDIENTS

Serves 4–6

2 medium onions, coarsely chopped

2 carrots, coarsely chopped

2 celery stalks, coarsely sliced

1 celery root, peeled and diced ½ inch

2 heads garlic, separated into cloves

3 pieces pork osso bucco, with a total weight of about 4 pounds

2½ cups beer

4 sage leaves for cooking

5 bay leaves

1 teaspoon salt

1 teaspoon black pepper, crushed

1 medium eggplant, cut into 1¼-inch slices

3 eggs, beaten

½ cup flour

Oil for frying

PREPARATION

1. In a baking pan, mix the onions, carrots, celery, celery root, garlic, meat, beer, sage leaves, bay leaves, salt, and pepper, and cover with aluminum foil.

2. Bake in the oven for 1½ hours at 350°F.

3. Soak the eggplant slices in egg, and then coat with flour. Fry in oil until lightly browned.

4. Remove the aluminum foil from the baking pan, add the eggplant slices, and mix gently.

5. Return to the oven and bake for about another hour at 350°F, until the meat is completely softened and browned.

6. Serve hot.

CHINESE EGGPLANT-BEEF FRY

*In this recipe, chicken or processed tofu (for those with vegetarian preferences)
may be substituted for the beef.*

INGREDIENTS

Serves 3–4

Caramel sauce (if you prefer not
to prepare the sauce, you can buy
golden syrup instead):

1 cup sugar

½ cup orange juice

Marinade:

1 tablespoon soy sauce

1 tablespoon brandy

1 tablespoon potato starch (or any
other type of starch)

1 egg white

Miscellaneous:

2 cups (approximately ¾ pound)
1½-inch long beef strips, sliced
against the grain of the beef

1 medium eggplant, sliced into
"finger" slices ½ inch thick

Coarse salt for salting eggplant

Oil for frying

2 cloves garlic, chopped

½ teaspoon ginger, chopped

1 tablespoon hot pepper sauce

2 tablespoons cooking oil

1 tablespoon of golden syrup or
caramel sauce (for preparation, see
below)

2 tablespoons soy sauce

1 tablespoon brandy

Pinch of salt

Pinch of pepper

1⅓ cups scallions, chopped

1 tablespoon sesame oil

PREPARATION

**Caramel sauce (if you choose to
prepare it yourself):**

1. Pour the sugar into a heated frying
pan in small amounts, gently stirring
with a wooden spoon to preserve the
light brown color.

2. Mix the orange juice, carefully and
gradually, into the sugar in the frying
pan.

Marinade:

1. Mix the marinade ingredients
together in a bowl. Place the beef
strips in the marinade.

3. Leave to marinate in the
refrigerator for 30 minutes.

To Assemble:

1. Sprinkle coarse salt over the
eggplant slices, and let sit for 20
minutes.

2. Shake the eggplant slices well to
remove any salt or fluid from them.

3. Deep-fry the eggplant slices in oil
until brown.

4. Remove from the frying pan and
leave to drain on paper towels.

5. Stir-fry the garlic, ginger, and hot
pepper sauce in a frying pan with
cooking oil.

6. Add the marinated beef strips and
stir-fry for 2–3 minutes.

7. Add the fried eggplant slices to the
frying pan and stir.

8. Gradually stir in the caramel sauce,
soy sauce, brandy, salt, and pepper,
and sauté for 2 to 3 minutes.

9. Transfer to a serving platter and
sprinkle the chopped scallion over it.
Sprinkle the sesame oil on top and
serve hot.

VEGETARIAN
ENTRÉES

SOBA NOODLES IN SPICY EGGPLANT SAUCE

This recipe makes a lovely sauce for rice or couscous as well as noodles.

INGREDIENTS

Serves 4–6

3 small thin eggplants (not pickling eggplants), sliced into ¾-inch rounds and halved

Coarse salt for salting eggplant

3 tablespoons peanut or sesame oil

¼ cup miso

½ cup chicken stock or vegetable stock

⅛ teaspoon cayenne pepper, or more to taste

1 tablespoon umeboshi (pickled plums) or balsamic vinegar

1 teaspoon orange zest

10⅔ ounces uncooked soba noodles

1 tablespoon scallion, chopped

PREPARATION

1. Sprinkle coarse salt over the eggplant slices, and let sit for 20 minutes.

2. Shake the eggplant slices well to remove any salt or fluid from them.

3. Heat the oil in a large pot and fry the eggplant until it is golden brown on one side. Flip the eggplant slices and fry on the other side for an additional 5 minutes until soft. Remove from heat.

4. Place the miso in a small saucepan with 2 tablespoons of stock, cayenne pepper, umeboshi (or vinegar), and the orange zest, and bring to a boil while stirring. Cook for 3 minutes and pour over the eggplant.

5. Cook the noodles according to the package directions and drain. Rinse well in cold water. Transfer the noodles to a large bowl.

6. Heat the remaining stock and pour over the noodles. Mix well.

7. Heat the sauce over a low flame and pour over the noodles. Mix carefully and garnish with scallion. Serve immediately.

FRIED EGGPLANT WITH TAHINI SAUCE

Tahini is a paste made from ground sesame seeds. It is a major ingredient in Middle Eastern recipes and can be purchased fresh, in cans, in jars, or dehydrated.

INGREDIENTS

Serves 4

5 cloves garlic, chopped

¼ cup olive oil

4 roasted medium eggplants, interior only

½ cup tahini paste

1⅓ cups parsley, chopped

1⅓ cups celery leaves, chopped

1 teaspoon salt

Pinch of black pepper

1 tablespoon pine nuts, roasted

PREPARATION

1. In a heavy frying pan, lightly fry the garlic in olive oil for 4–5 minutes.

2. Add the eggplant and tahini and fry for about 5 more minutes.

3. Add the parsley and celery, and season with salt and pepper.

4. Transfer to a platter, garnish with the pine nuts, and serve hot.

TURKISH EGGPLANT FAN

The eggplant fan is a simple but tasty dish which goes well with a healthy green salad and bread.

INGREDIENTS

Serves 2

1 medium eggplant

Coarse salt for salting eggplant

1 egg, well beaten

Pinch of salt

½ cup flour

Oil for frying

PREPARATION

1. Peel the eggplant.

2. Slice the eggplant into 3 slices, from bottom to top, leaving the tops of the slices connected together.

3. Arrange the connected slices in a fan pattern.

4. Sprinkle coarse salt over the eggplant slices, and let sit for 20 minutes.

5. Shake the eggplant slices well to remove any salt or fluid from them.

6. Coat the slices with egg and salt, and then with flour.

7. Deep-fry over a medium flame until brown and soft.

8. Leave to drain on paper towels.

9. Serve hot with yogurt sauce and diced tomatoes, or lemon juice.

EGGPLANT NOODLE AND TOFU CASSEROLE

This is a rich vegetarian dish which is easy to prepare, and, for those who prefer it, chicken may be substituted for the tofu.

INGREDIENTS

Serves 4

1 medium eggplant, sliced into ½-inch strips

Oil for baking and frying

1 onion, chopped

1 carrot, sliced lengthwise

1 teaspoon fresh ginger, chopped

1 tablespoon garlic, crushed

⅓ cup roasted peanuts, coarsely chopped

1 cup broccoli florets, scalded for 2 minutes in boiling water

1 cup tofu, sliced into strips

2 tablespoons sesame oil

5 scallions, chopped

6 cups cooked rice noodles

4 tablespoons soy sauce

1 tablespoon sweet chili sauce

PREPARATION

1. Spread oil over the eggplant slices and place in a baking pan.

2. Bake in the oven for 20 minutes at 350°F.

3. In a deep frying pan, fry the onion and carrot until medium brown.

4. Add the ginger and garlic and quick-fry.

5. Add the peanuts, broccoli, tofu, and sesame oil, and mix together.

6. Add the scallion, eggplant slices, and rice noodles, and sauté lightly.

7. Add the soy sauce and chili sauce and sauté again.

8. Serve hot.

VEGETARIAN TOFU MOUSSAKA

Tofu moussaka is a delicious vegetarian dish popular among meat eaters as well.
The only difference between this dish and meat moussaka is the filling which is
very satisfying and easy to digest.

INGREDIENTS

Serves 6–8

3 large eggplants, peeled and sliced into ¾-inch slices

Coarse salt for salting eggplant

Oil for frying

1 large onion, thinly chopped

⅓ cup olive oil

1 egg, beaten

1 cup parsley, chopped

2 cups tofu, chopped

1 cup salted cheese, crumbled

Pinch of pepper

6 tomatoes, diced ¼ inch

Batter made from 2 eggs, beaten well with 1 tablespoon of flour and a pinch of salt and pepper

PREPARATION

1. Sprinkle coarse salt over the eggplant slices, and let sit for 40 minutes.

2. Shake the eggplant slices well to remove any salt or fluid from them.

3. Partially fry the eggplant slices in oil until lightly browned, and leave to drain on paper towels.

4. Fry the onion in olive oil in a frying pan until brown, then cool.

5. Mix together the onion, egg, parsley, tofu, salted cheese, and pepper in a bowl to complete the filling.

6. Line the base and the walls of a Pyrex baking pan with half of the eggplant slices.

7. Pour the filling on top of the eggplant slices, and spread the tomatoes over it.

8. Cover with a layer of the remaining eggplant slices, and pour the batter over that.

9. Cover with aluminum foil and bake in the oven at 350°F for 40 minutes.

10. Remove the aluminum foil and continue baking for another 15 minutes.

11. Serve hot or reheated on the day after its preparation.

EGGPLANT BEAN STEW

Enjoy this hearty, nutritious, and filling dish on a cold winter's day.

INGREDIENTS

Serves 6

½ cup lentils, soaked overnight

¾ cup kidney beans, soaked overnight

2 medium eggplants, sliced into 1-inch slices

Oil for frying

2 onions, chopped

2 carrots, coarsely sliced

½ cup olive oil

1 celery root (or celeriac as it is sometimes called), grated

1 parsley root, grated

1 teaspoon salt

1 tablespoon paprika

2 tablespoons brown sugar

½ cup tomato paste

6 cups vegetable stock

½ cup coriander or parsley, chopped

PREPARATION

1. Cook the lentils and kidney beans in water in separate pots until completely soft (about 40 minutes for lentils, and 3 hours for kidney beans) and drain.

2. Fry the eggplant slices in oil until lightly browned, and leave to drain on paper towels.

3. In a pot, fry the onion and carrots in olive oil until browned.

4. Add the celery root and parsley root, and quick-fry.

5. Add the salt, paprika, brown sugar, and tomato paste, and mix in.

6. Pour in vegetable stock and bring to a boil.

7. Reduce the flame and add in the kidney beans, lentils, and fried eggplant.

8. Cook over medium flame for 30 minutes.

9. Pour into a serving dish, sprinkle coriander or parsley on top, and serve hot.

EGGPLANT RISOTTO

The eggplant and dried tomatoes in this recipe give the creamy risotto a distinct kick.

INGREDIENTS

Serves 2–3

1 medium eggplant, diced ½ inch

⅓ cup olive oil

1 red onion, finely chopped

Oil for frying

1 cup Italian risotto rice

¼ cup dry white wine

3½ cups chicken or vegetable stock

¼ cup dried tomatoes, coarsely sliced

½ teaspoon salt

Pinch of pepper

1 tomato, diced

⅓ cup parsley, chopped

1 tablespoon butter

2 tablespoons Parmesan cheese, grated

PREPARATION

1. Mix the diced eggplant with olive oil, and bake in the oven for 20 minutes at 350°F.

2. In a deep frying pan, fry the onion with a small amount of oil until lightly brown.

3. Add the rice, wine, and half of the chicken or vegetable stock, and cook over a medium flame while stirring constantly until the liquid is absorbed.

4. Add the dried tomatoes and stir.

5. Gradually stir in the remaining chicken or vegetable stock until the liquid is absorbed.

6. Season with salt and pepper, and add the eggplant, tomato, parsley, butter, and cheese, and stir well.

7. Serve hot.

BULGARIAN EGGPLANT

Since this dish is served at room temperature, you can prepare it in advance, refrigerate it, and remove it from the refrigerator a couple of hours before serving it. It also preserves its flavor for several days.

INGREDIENTS

Serves 4

1 onion, thinly sliced

2 red peppers, thinly sliced

4 carrots, grated

⅓ cup oil for frying

1 cup rice

1 level teaspoon salt

Pinch of pepper

1½ cups water

Oil for greasing baking pan and sprinkling on top

2 large eggplants, halved and emptied of their flesh

2 tomatoes, sliced into ½-inch slices

PREPARATION

1. In a pot, fry the onion, peppers, and carrots in oil until the onions reach transparency.

2. Add the rice and quick-fry.

3. Add the salt, pepper, and water, and bring to a boil.

4. Cover the pot, reduce the flame, and cook for 20 minutes.

5. Turn off the flame and leave the pot covered for 10 more minutes.

6. Grease the baking pan and place the eggplant halves in it.

7. Fill each eggplant half with an equal amount of rice and vegetables from the pot, and cover with 2–3 tomato slices.

8. Pour some oil on top, and bake in the oven for 40 minutes at 325°F.

9. Serve at room temperature.

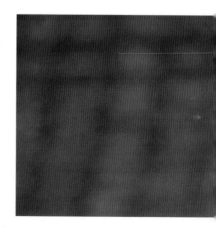

BEER-BATTERED EGGPLANT

Deep-frying eggplant in beer batter produces light, golden, fluffy, and crisp results.

INGREDIENTS

Serves 4–6

1 medium eggplant, sliced into thin (¼-inch) slices

Coarse salt for salting eggplant

Cooking oil

Batter:

1 cup regular flour or rice flour

2 cups beer

⅓ cup coriander, chopped

⅓ cup parsley, chopped

1 thyme sprig, chopped

1 teaspoon brown sugar

PREPARATION

1. Mix together all the batter ingredients in a bowl until a uniform texture is achieved.

2. Sprinkle coarse salt over the eggplant, and let sit for 20 minutes.

3. Shake the eggplant slices well to remove any salt or fluid from them.

4. Dip the eggplant slices in the batter.

5. Deep-fry the eggplant in a pan pre-heated to medium heat until golden brown.

6. Leave to drain on paper towels.

7. Serve hot.

ROASTED EGGPLANT AND MUSHROOM MEDALLIONS

These wonderful patties are perfect for an entrée or as a side dish.

INGREDIENTS

Makes 6 patties

3 medium eggplants, scorched

¼ cup olive oil

1 large onion, finely chopped

½ pound champignon mushrooms, finely chopped

2 red potatoes, washed, peeled and finely grated

7 ounces hard goat cheese, finely grated

½ cup parsley, chopped

1 egg

4 tablespoons flour

Salt to taste

Freshly ground black pepper to taste

Cooking oil

PREPARATION

1. Scoop the meat out of the cooked eggplants and place in a colander to drain for 2 hours. Squeeze the meat in your hands to extract all the juice and then set aside in a bowl.

2. Heat the olive oil in a heavy-bottomed skillet. Add the onions and cook until golden brown. Add the mushrooms and cook until all the liquid is evaporated. Transfer to the bowl with the eggplant.

3. Add the grated potatoes to the eggplant mixture. Add the cheese, parsley, egg, flour, salt, and pepper. Mix well. Add more flour as necessary to create a uniform batter.

4. Heat some oil in a large skillet. Flour your hands and form patties from the batter. Fry each patty until both sides are golden brown. Remove from skillet and place on paper towels to drain. Serve hot.

ORIENTAL EGGPLANT FRY

This dish is actually of Middle Eastern origin, and is also appropriate as a side dish with pasta or salty pastries.

INGREDIENTS

Serves 6

2 medium eggplants, sliced into "finger" slices, 1 inch thick

Cooking oil

2 tablespoons ground garlic

3 heaping tablespoons tomato paste

1 teaspoon cumin

1 teaspoon hot paprika

1 teaspoon sweet paprika

½ teaspoon turmeric

1 teaspoon chicken or vegetable soup mix

2 teaspoons brown sugar

½ teaspoon salt

⅓ cup scallions, chopped

1⅓ cups coriander, chopped

¾ cup water

PREPARATION

1. Spread the oil thinly over the eggplant slices. Broil in the oven for 25 minutes at 350°F.

2. Fry the garlic in a small amount of oil in a pot over a high flame until golden brown.

3. Add the tomato paste, cumin, hot paprika, sweet paprika, turmeric, soup mix, brown sugar, and salt, and quick fry.

4. Add all the other ingredients (including the eggplant slices) and stir gently.

5. Cover the pot and reduce the flame, and continue cooking for another 15 minutes.

6. Serve at room temperature.

EGGPLANT SPAGHETTINI ALI OLIO

Ali olio is one of the most popular Italian pasta sauces. Though eggplant is generally not a part of this dish, we have integrated it into this recipe to create a truly unique and dazzling concoction.

INGREDIENTS

Serves 4

1 large eggplant, diced ½ inch

Coarse salt for salting eggplant

Cooking oil

¾ cup olive oil

6 cloves garlic, sliced

Pinch of dry ground chili

Handful chopped parsley

One-pound package of spaghettini noodles, cooked in water according to the instructions on the package (generally, for 8 minutes)

½ cup Parmesan cheese, grated

PREPARATION

1. Sprinkle coarse salt over the eggplant, and let sit for 20 minutes.

2. Rinse the eggplant well to remove any salt or fluid.

3. Deep-fry the eggplant until brown and soft.

4. Leave to drain on paper towels.

5. Pour the olive oil into a wide frying pan, and fry the garlic until golden brown.

6. Add the eggplant, chili, and parsley, and sauté lightly.

7. Add the spaghettini and sauté lightly.

8. Sprinkle the Parmesan cheese on top and serve hot.

SAUCES
AND JAMS

BALSAM AND GINGER EGGPLANT JAM

This recipe serves as an excellent antipasto and it keeps in the refrigerator for up to a week.

INGREDIENTS

Makes approximately ½ pound of jam

1 large eggplant, sliced into ½-inch slices

Coarse salt for salting eggplant

Oil for frying

1½ cups balsamic vinegar

1 cup brown sugar

1 teaspoon fresh ginger, chopped

3 cloves garlic, sliced

PREPARATION

1. Sprinkle coarse salt over the eggplant slices, and let sit for 20 minutes.

2. Shake the eggplant slices well to remove any salt or fluid from them.

3. Fry the eggplant slices in oil until browned and softened.

4. Leave to drain on paper towels.

5. In a frying pan over a high flame, reduce the balsamic vinegar with brown sugar, ginger, and garlic, until only half of the liquid remains.

6. Add the eggplant slices to the pan with balsamic vinegar. Mix together and leave over a medium flame for about 5 minutes.

7. Store in a storage container after cooling (though it may also be used hot).

SAFFRON EGGPLANT JAM

This jam is perfect for serving with aged cheeses, and is also a good accompaniment for courses containing liver.

INGREDIENTS

Makes approximately ½ pound of jam

1 medium eggplant, sliced into 1-inch strips

⅓ cup oil

Syrup:

1½ cups sugar

1 cup water

1 cup lemon juice

A pinch of saffron

Pinch of lemon zest, grated

PREPARATION

1. Spread oil over the eggplant strips, and bake in the oven for 20 minutes at 350°F.

2. Pour all the syrup ingredients into a pot and cook over a medium flame, stirring frequently.

3. Add the eggplant strips to a pot with syrup. Stir and cook over a low flame for 5 more minutes.

4. Store in a storage container and cool.

FETA EGGPLANT SAUCE

This makes a wonderful sauce to top bruschetta.

INGREDIENTS

Serves 6

2 medium eggplants, roasted, peeled, and torn into strips by hand or with a fork

1 cube feta cheese

2 cloves garlic

⅓ cup olive oil

Small amount olive oil for seasoning

PREPARATION

Mash all the ingredien together with a woode fork until the mixture is smooth and uniform. Season with olive oil to taste.

EGGPLANT CARBONARA

In Italian, Carbonara means "coal"; it is believed that the coal miners were the first ones to use this sauce.

INGREDIENTS

2 servings

cooking oil

cup bacon, diced ½ inch

small eggplant, diced ½ inch

2 cups sweet cream

½ teaspoon ground black pepper

4 egg yolks

PREPARATION

1. Grease a baking pan with oil, and combine the bacon and eggplant and place in a baking pan.

2. Roast in the oven at 350°F for 20 minutes, stirring from time to time.

3. In a frying pan, reduce the cream and pepper for 5 minutes while stirring, leaving about ⅓ the amount of liquid.

4. Add the eggplant and bacon to the frying pan, and cool for 2 minutes. Gradually mix in the egg yolks.

5. Serve over pasta.

EGGPLANT AND KASHKAVAL CHEESE CREAM SAUCE

Kashkaval is a semi-firm cheese made from sheep's milk. It is a available at most fine cheese shops and delis. If you wish, you may substitute provolone or mozzarella cheese.

INGREDIENTS

2 servings

1 medium eggplant

1 cup sweet cream

¼ cup white wine

¼ teaspoon ground black pepper

5 basil leaves, sliced into strips

3 tablespoons kashkaval cheese, grated

1 tomato, diced

PREPARATION

1. Scorch the eggplant thoroughly over an open flame, or in a frying pan, to char the skin and soften the flesh.

2. Cool and scoop the flesh from the eggplant peel.

3. Pour the cream, wine, and pepper into a frying pan, and reduce over a high flame for 5 minutes, while stirring to prevent the sauce from boiling over.

4. Add the eggplant flesh, basil, cheese, and tomato; stir and reduce over a medium flame for 5 minutes.

5. Pour over the pasta or baked potato while hot.

INDEX